BLASTOFF! READERS, AN IMPRINT OF BELLWETHER MEDIA BY FLUTTERBEE

Blastoff! Readers are carefully developed by literacy experts to build reading stamina and move students toward fluency by combining standards-based content with developmentally appropriate text.

Level 1 provides the most support through repetition of high-frequency words, light text, predictable sentence patterns, and strong visual support.

Level 2 offers early readers a bit more challenge through varied sentences, increased text load, and text-supportive special features.

Level 3 advances early-fluent readers toward fluency through increased text load, less reliance on photos, advancing concepts, longer sentences, and more complex special features.

★ **Blastoff! Universe**

Reading Level

Grade K

Grades 1–3

Grade 4

This edition first published in 2027 by Bellwether Media, Inc.

For information regarding permission, write to Bellwether Media, Inc., Attention: Permissions Department, 3500 American Blvd W, Suite 150, Bloomington, MN 55431.

Library of Congress Cataloging-in-Publication Data

Names: James, India author
Title: Astrobiologist / India James.
Description: Minneapolis, Minnesota : Bellwether Media, Inc, 2027. | Series: Careers in STEM | Includes bibliographical references and index. | Audience: Ages 5-8 | Audience: Grades 2-3 | Summary: "Simple text and full-color photography introduce beginning readers to astrobiologists. Developed by literacy experts for students in kindergarten through third grade"– Provided by publisher.
Identifiers: LCCN 2026010736 (print) | LCCN 2026010737 (ebook) | ISBN 9798898800758 (library binding) | ISBN 9798898801991 (ebook)
Subjects: LCSH: Exobiology | Space biology | Exobiology–Vocational guidance | Space biology–Vocational guidance
Classification: LCC QH326 .J36 2026 (print) | LCC QH326 (ebook)
LC record available at https://lccn.loc.gov/2026010736
LC ebook record available at https://lccn.loc.gov/2026010737

Editor: Betsy Rathburn   Designer: Andrea Schneider

Printed in the United States of America, North Mankato, MN.

Table of Contents

Finding Life

The clock counts down.
When it hits zero,
the rocket blasts off!
It is headed to Mars.

The rocket carries
many tools.
Astrobiologists will use
them to look for life.

tool being
used on Mars

rocket

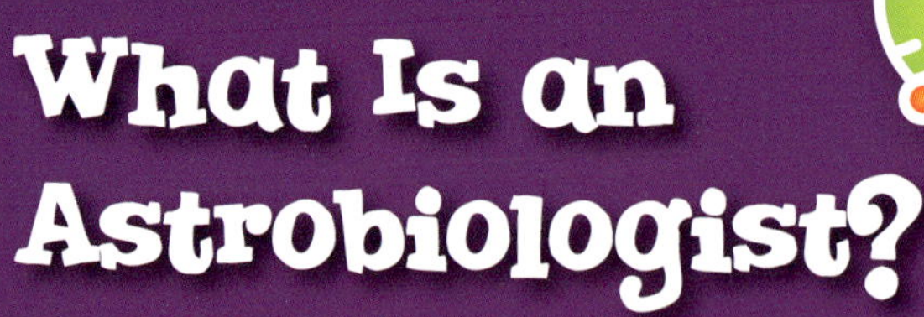

What Is an Astrobiologist?

An astrobiologist is a type of scientist. They study life in the **universe**.

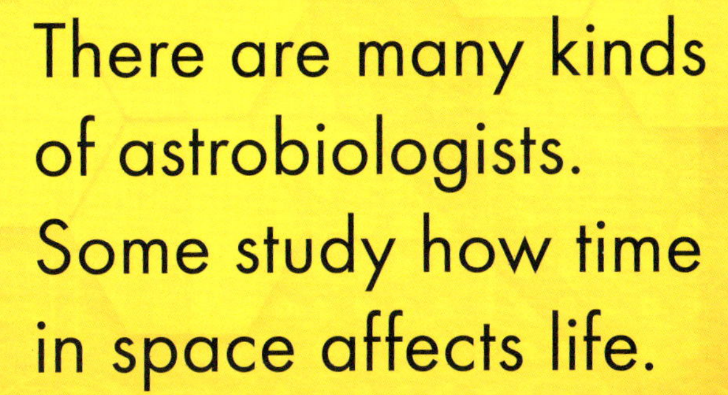

There are many kinds of astrobiologists. Some study how time in space affects life.

Some study whether life exists beyond Earth. They look for signs in the **chemicals** on other planets.

Famous Astrobiologist

Name	Lynn Margulis
Born	March 5, 1938
Died	November 22, 2011
Birthplace	Chicago, Illinois
Schooling	University of Chicago; University of Wisconsin–Madison; University of California, Berkeley
Known For	new ideas about how life on Earth formed and changed

Others study Earth. This helps them ask questions about how life may form on other planets.

At Work

Astrobiologists work in **labs** and offices. They look at **data** about life. They study **samples**.

They also use data from robots and **satellites** in space. They use computers and **microscopes** to study data.

Astrobiology in Real Life

new tools to visit extreme places

new tools to discover signs of life

better understanding of Earth

Some astrobiologists work outside to study Earth. They go to places deep underwater. They look at places with extreme weather.

They **compare** extreme places on Earth to places in space. They want to see where life could exist.

astrobiologist in Antarctica

place in Spain
with extreme
weather

Some astrobiologists are also **journalists**. They explain their findings to people.

zucchini plant in space

Others study life in space. They may send living things to space. They look at how **gravity** affects life.

Becoming an Astrobiologist

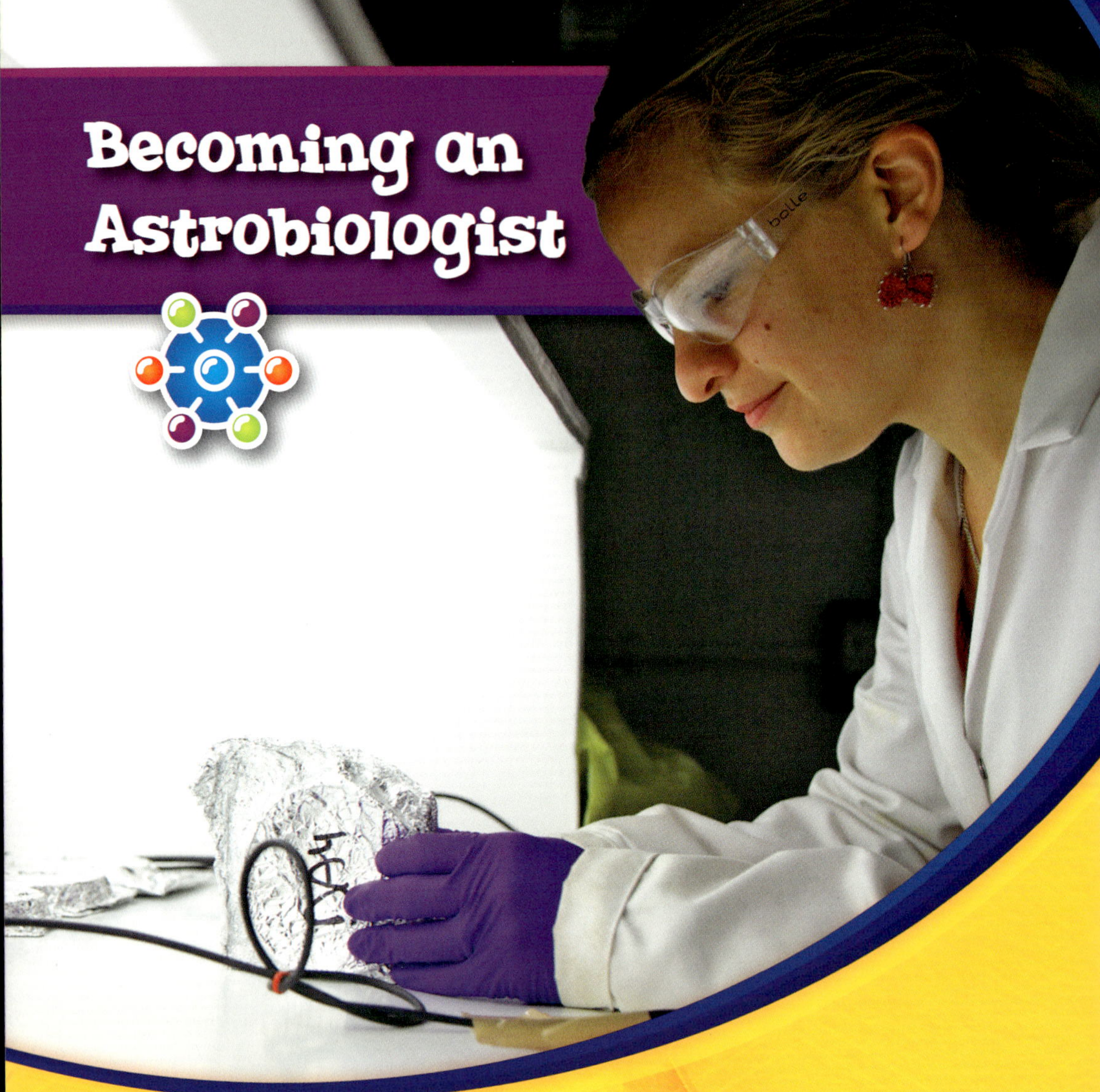

Astrobiologists study science in college. They take classes in **biology** and **chemistry**.

They often go to **graduate school**. They do **research**. They learn more about a subject.

Using STEM

Science — ask questions about life in the universe

Technology — use computers to answer questions

Engineering — make robots to gather data

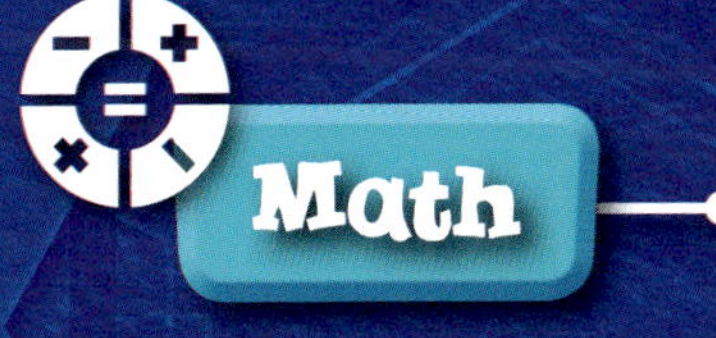

Math — measure chemicals on other planets to look for life

Astrobiologists also learn as they work. They work with more experienced astrobiologists. They learn skills for each job.

Many astrobiologists work in labs. They may lead their own lab one day.

Astrobiologists are good at asking questions. They use data to test their **theories**. They must be good researchers.

How to Become an Astrobiologist

1. study science in college
2. choose a subject to study further in graduate school
3. get a job at a lab, news organization, or museum
4. work with expert astrobiologists

Being an astrobiologist is an interesting job!

Glossary

biology—a science that deals with things that are alive

chemicals—materials that can cause a change in other materials

chemistry—a science that deals with substances and the changes they go through

compare—to note how alike or different things are

data—information

graduate school—a school where people study a specialty area after college

gravity—the force that pulls objects toward one another

journalists—people who report news

labs—buildings or rooms with special tools to do science experiments and tests

microscopes—tools used for looking at very small things

research—careful study to learn new information

samples—small amounts of things that give information about where they were taken from

satellites—human-made objects that circle Earth

theories—ideas that try to explain something

universe—all of space and everything in it, including planets, stars, and galaxies

To Learn More

AT THE LIBRARY

Florance, Cara. *The Space Science Handbook: 32 Celestial Science Projects for Kids*. Naperville, Ill.: Sourcebooks eXplore, 2025.

Hand, Carol. *Living in Space*. New York, N.Y.: PowerKids Press, 2021.

Lombardo, Jennifer. *The James Webb Space Telescope*. Buffalo, N.Y.: PowerKids Press, 2025.

ON THE WEB

FACTSURFER

Factsurfer.com gives you a safe, fun way to find more information.

1. Go to www.factsurfer.com.
2. Enter "astrobiologist" into the search box and click 🔍.
3. Select your book cover to see a list of related content.

Index

The images in this book are reproduced through the courtesy of: gorodenkoff, front cover (astrobiologist); Alican, front cover (space); Agata, front cover (satellite); Johanna, p. 3; NASA/ JPL-Caltech/ Olivier de Goursac/ Wikipedia, p. 4 (tool); Joel Kowsky/ Wikipedia, pp. 4-5; JAVIER SORIANO/ Contributor/ Getty Images, pp. 6-7 (top); NG Images/ Alamy, pp. 7, 18 (inset); Jpedreira/ Wikipedia, p. 8 (Margulis); NASA/ ZUMA Wire, pp. 8-9; NASA Goddard Space Flight Center/ Wikipedia, pp. 10-11 (lab); Andrei Armiagov, p. 10 (satellite); NASA/ JPL-Caltech/ Wikipedia, p. 11 (extreme places); NASA/ Jet Propulsion Laboratory/ Wikipedia, p. 11 (signs of life); NASA/ Ames Research Center/ Abby Tabor, p. 11 (Earth); Dawn Y Sumner/ Wikipedia, p. 12 (Antarctica); Octavio Passos/ Contributor/ Getty Images, pp. 12-13 (Spain); Dominika Zarzycka/ NurPhoto, p. 14; Donald Pettit/ Wikipedia, pp. 14-15 (zucchini); Adam685/ Wikipedia, pp. 16-17; skynesher, pp. 18-19; BillionPhotos.com, pp. 20-21 (bottom); NASA Goddard Space Flight Center/ Molly Wasser/ Wikipedia, pp. 20-21 (top); NASA/ JPL-Caltech/ MSSS/ Wikipedia, pp. 22-23.